KIND AGAIN

How to Return to Kindness
like Dolly Parton

Kennadee Fabin

Published by Dadvice TV

To my Dad,

You've always been my biggest cheerleader and the one who taught me about the power of being kind and strong. You're the reason I felt brave enough to write this book and share my thoughts with the world. Every time I wrote a page, I thought of all the cool stories and lessons you've shared with me. Thanks for being the best dad ever. This book is for you, and I hope it makes you as proud as I am to be your kid!

Love,
Kennadee

CONTENTS

FOREWORD

In today's noisy world, where people often argue and disagree, a special young girl named Kennadee stands out. At just 11 years old, she's a big fan of Dolly Parton and has a big message to share: let's be kind to each other. Growing up during the Covid Pandemic, Kennadee saw many people fighting - on TV, in stores, and even in schools. She didn't like it. So, she decided to do something about it. She wanted to remind everyone how to be friendly and kind because it seemed like some people had forgotten. With this book, Kennadee shares her message of making friends and being good to one another. I'm her dad, and I couldn't be prouder. She's put so much hard work into this book, and because of it, she's become one of the youngest authors in Michigan. For everyone reading this, I hope you see all the hard work and love Kennadee put into her book. I hope it reminds you that even when things get tough, we can still be kind to one another. And sometimes, it's the youngest among us, like Kennadee, who show us the way.

With a lot of pride and love,

James Fabin

ABOUT ME

My name is Kennadee Fabin, and I was born on the spookiest day of the year. I bet you guessed it, Halloween! I am 11 years old, and I absolutely love butterflies! They are just so majestic and free. It's like they have no thoughts and are just calmly gliding around in the sky.

But you know what else is cool? Dolly Parton! My awesome dad introduced her to me, just like other good country singers like Reba McEntire and Trace Atkins. Of Course, my dad has all of Dolly's songs in his playlist so it wasn't long before I heard one of her songs. I immediately loved them. The first one I ever heard was *Coat of Many Colors*. Then I started learning all of the words to her songs.

They are so good they can easily get stuck in your head. I would start humming them when I brush my teeth, and when I'm doing my homework. Some of my favorite songs are, *"Love is like a Butterfly"*, *"9 to 5"*, *"Jolene"*, and *"Coat of Many Colors."*

My dad is kind of like Dolly because he helps people with kidney disease every day with his YouTube channel. He also has two books, and he's the one who gave me the idea to write a book too.

I try to be just as kind and loving as Dolly when I meet someone new, I try to be their friend right away. If someone's feeling left out, or if they're different, I make it a point to include them. Everyone deserves a friend, don't they?

And that's what Dolly Parton is all about. Being kind, spreading love, and embracing everyone, no matter how different they are. She's shown me how much better the world can be when we're kind to each other. And I want to share that message with the world!

Where I'm from
House #1: Seattle, Washington
I am from a backyard full of joyful dogs
with blackberry and raspberry bushes
along the wooden fence
and a great big apple tree towering
over the other trees

House #2 : West Chester, Ohio
I am from a 2-story house with a
creaking trampoline
With lots of plants and good food,
sweet Nutella crepes,
Crunchy Sabritones, and grandma's
homemade potato candy

House #3 : Symmes Township, Ohio
A house surrounded by kind friends, on all sides

With fun activities for all of the holidays
And lots of different pets from dogs to ducks
So many play structures in all of the big backyards

House #4 : Farmington Hills, Michigan
I am from a house with a stream
flowing through the front yard
With cottonwood trees swaying in
the wind behind my house
We go on long road trips to different
towns, states, and countries

WHO IS DOLLY PARTON?

Let's learn more about Dolly Parton. She is a real life superstar, but what I love most about her is how she shines from the inside out. She's like a sparkly butterfly that adds color to everything around her!

Dolly Parton was born in a tiny little cabin in the Great Smoky Mountains of Tennessee. She was the fourth of twelve children. Can you imagine having eleven brothers and sisters? Dolly's family didn't have a lot of money, but they sure had a lot of love. And they had music. Dolly started singing almost as soon as she could talk. She even made her first guitar out of an old mandolin and some twine. She's been making music ever since, and her songs have touched the hearts of millions of people around the world.

Her voice is like sweet honey, strong and smooth. She sings about real things, about life and love, about dreams and hard work. Songs like "Jolene" and "Coat of Many Colors" tell stories from her life. When you listen to her songs, you can feel what she feels, and it's like she's right there with you. Her music brings comfort and joy to so many people. It's like a warm hug from a friend.

But Dolly Parton isn't just a singer and songwriter, she's also an actress! She's been in a bunch of movies, like "9 to 5" and "Steel Magnolias". These movies are so much fun to watch! Dolly brings her bright, sparkly personality to every role she plays. You can't help but love her!

Did you know that Dolly Parton even has her own theme park? It's called Dollywood! Just imagine roller coasters and water rides, music and shows, all in one place! And all of it is full of Dolly's love and kindness. Visiting Dollywood is one of my biggest dreams. I daydream about riding the roller coasters and listening to live country music. But you know what's even cooler? I don't just want to visit Dollywood. I dream about working there one day!

One of the most amazing things about Dollywood isn't the rides or the shows, it's how much Dolly cares about the people who work there. She believes in helping people learn and grow. That's why she started the Dollywood scholarship program. This program gives money to employees who want to go to college. Isn't that awesome? Dolly knows that education is a key to unlocking your dreams. She's using her success to help others succeed. That's just another reason why I think she's so amazing.

To me Dolly Parton is way more than a star. She's a

guide, a light that shows us that we can be whatever we dream to be. She teaches us to be kind, to dream big, and to never forget where we come from. She's a real life hero, and I hope that as you read this book, you'll come to love her as much as I do!

Dolly Parton's history

I want to tell you all about Dolly Parton's life, starting from when she was just a little girl. Her story makes me believe that if you have a dream and you work hard, you can make it come true. Here's how she did it.

When Dolly was just a little kid, she started to play the guitar. She even wrote her own songs. She'd sing for anyone who'd listen, her family, her neighbors, and even people at the store! I think that's super cool.

When she graduated high school, she knew she wanted to be a big country music star. So, she went to Nashville. That's where all the big country singers go. She sang on TV, and she met a guy named Porter Wagoner. He was already a star, and he helped her get started.

But Dolly had big dreams. She wanted to write her own songs and sing them herself. She wanted to be her own star. So, she worked really, really hard. And guess what? People loved her! She made albums and went on tours, and everyone wanted to hear her sing.

Dolly's songs were special, like growing up poor and having dreams. People could feel what she was saying. Like her song "Coat of Many Colors." It's about a coat her momma made her. It was all different colors because they couldn't afford new fabric, but it was made with love. That song makes me think of Dolly's whole life.

Her life wasn't always easy, but she never gave up. Now she's super famous. She's been in movies, wrote lots of songs, and she has her own theme park called Dollywood.

One of my favorite things about Dolly is that she never forgot where she came from. She loves her family and her mountain home. And she helps other people too. She gives money to schools and hospitals, and she even helps kids get books with her imagination library.

Dolly Parton's life is like one of her songs. It's happy and sad, it's fun, and it's real. It's about dreams coming true. Her story makes me feel like I can do anything if I believe in myself. Just like Dolly, I have big dreams, and I'm ready to chase them. Maybe one day, I'll meet her at Dollywood! That's one of my dreams. What's one of yours?

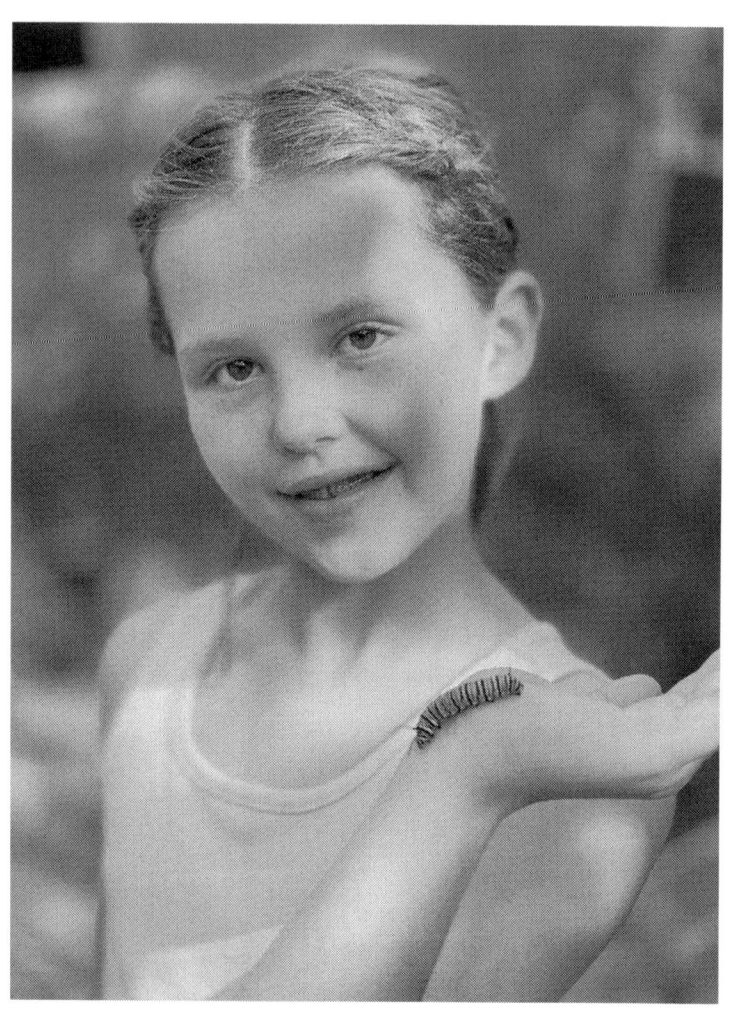

WHY I'M WRITING THIS BOOK

I'm writing this book so that people can be more like Dolly. I'm not saying that there are no other great role models in this world, but Dolly is a great example. In the next chapter you can see how you can be a great person just like Dolly.

One day, my dad and I were driving for 5 whole hours to visit some of my friends back in Cincinnati, Ohio. You see, I had moved to Detroit, Michigan, a year ago, and we often make the long trip to see my old friends.

Every time we get close to the neighborhood in Cincinnati, we do something really special. We roll all the windows down, open the sunroof, and play the song "Return to Innocence" by Enigma super loud! The wind rushes into the car, and my dad and I both put an arm out the window, riding the wind with our hands. We're totally in sync with each other, singing really loud, and feeling free and happy.

And that's when it hit me!

I knew right then what I would name my book: "Kind Again." I wanted to capture that magical feeling my dad and I shared and the love and happiness we felt in that moment. It was like returning to a time when everything was pure and good, just like in the song.

So, I decided the subtitle would be "Return to Kindness Like Dolly Parton." Because that's what Dolly does, isn't it? She makes people feel kind again. She takes us back to that place where everyone is nice to each other, just like the way my dad and I feel when we're singing our favorite song on the road back to Cincinnati.

I hope that when you read this book, you'll feel that same joy and kindness that my dad and I share on our special trips. And maybe, just maybe, you'll be inspired to be kind again, too, just like Dolly.

WHAT IS KINDNESS?

Have you ever watched little kids at a park? They just walk up to each other, maybe share a toy or start a game, and within minutes, they're laughing and playing as if they've been friends forever. They don't worry about what someone looks like or where they come from. They just want to have fun and make a new buddy. That, right there, is the heart of kindness.

Kindness is like a special magic inside of us that makes the world a better place. It's that warm feeling you get when you do something good for someone else, even if it's just a tiny thing. It's like a little spark inside of us, always ready to light up someone's day.

When we talk about kindness, we're not just talking about big things, like giving someone a huge present. Kindness can be in the small things too. Like sharing your snack, helping someone with their homework, or just listening when a friend wants to talk.

Do you know what's super cool about kindness? We're all born with it! Just like how we're born knowing how to laugh or cry, we're also born with the ability to be kind. That's why little kids are so good at making friends. They use their natural kindness without even thinking about it.

But as we get older, sometimes life gets more complicated. We start to notice differences. Maybe someone dresses differently, has a different accent, or comes from a different country. Sometimes, these differences make us unsure or even scared. But guess what? Kindness doesn't care about these differences. Kindness just wants to connect and spread happiness.

Being kind doesn't mean you have to agree with everyone or like everything they do. But it does mean understanding that every person has feelings. And every person deserves respect and care.

Think about a time when you felt sad, and someone showed you kindness. Maybe they gave you a hug, told a joke to make you laugh, or just sat with you. That act of kindness probably felt like a warm blanket on a cold day.

So, what is kindness? It's that magic inside of us, ready to make the world shine brighter. And the more we practice it, the better we get at it.

Always remember, you have a superpower – the

power of kindness. Use it every day, and watch the
world around you change for the better!

REASONS DOLLY IS A GREAT PERSON

Kindness Everywhere
Dolly's heart must be made of gold. She's kind to everyone. People, animals, strangers. She loves them all! And you know what's really cool? She's all about sharing and caring. Like giving a million dollars to help find a cure for a really bad sickness. That's like superhero stuff!

Helping Others
I wish there were more people like Dolly in the world. She has a program called Dolly's Library that gives FREE books to kids. She knows that reading is super important, so she helps kids get books, especially those who don't have extra money for the newest ones. It's like she's planting seeds of dreams in their minds. I love that!

Inclusiveness
Dolly's all about making friends and being nice to

everyone, no matter where they come from. Just like me! One time, I saw a kid at the playground that others wouldn't play with. She looked lonely. Like Dolly, I went up and introduced myself. Guess what? She was just shy, and we became great new friends! I totally agree with Dolly, everyone should feel like they belong.

Positivity

Have you ever heard Dolly's laugh? It's like sunshine! She makes everyone feel good with her smile and her positive words. When I feel down, I listen to her songs, and I feel like dancing again. She's like a big sister, telling you that everything's gonna be alright.

Helping People Learn

Guess what? Dolly helps people who work at Dollywood get scholarships to go to college. Isn't that amazing? But that's not all! She also started Dolly's Library, which provides free books to kids to help them enjoy reading. She wants everyone to learn and follow their dreams. She makes the world a smarter place.

Her Love for Butterflies

Dolly loves butterflies, just like me! She says they remind her of dreams, and that's what her songs are about. She thinks we can all spread our wings and fly. Isn't that a pretty thought?

So there you have it! Dolly Parton is a great person because she's kind, helps others, includes everyone, and fills the world with positivity. She's like a big, warm hug. I want to be like her when I grow up. Let's all be a little more like Dolly, and the world will be a happier place.

What do you think? Let's go spread some kindness!

WHY THE WORLD NEEDS MORE PEOPLE LIKE DOLLY!

When I'm at home and my dad listens to the news, I can't help but overhear people fighting and not getting along all around the world. It's everywhere! It's like they're playing a never-ending game of tug-of-war, but no one's winning.

I wonder how they got to be this way. I bet these people were once kids who played together in the sandbox, on the playground, or at the park. They would have been really good friends, sharing snacks, telling jokes, and even getting into little scrapes together.

But then something changed. They grew up and somehow forgot how to start with kindness and openness. They forgot how cool it was to discover how different people can be and still be friends. They

21

stopped seeing the differences between them as exciting ways to learn about each other and started seeing them as reasons to fight.

Now, they argue about things that I think they could figure out if they just talked and listened. Instead of saying, "You're different, and that's bad," they could say, "You're different, tell me more!" If someone likes one thing and someone else likes another, that doesn't mean they can't still be friends. It means they can teach each other something new.

But what if more people were like Dolly Parton? Imagine how awesome that would be!

Dolly is never afraid to be herself, and she thinks it's great when others are themselves too. She doesn't see differences as problems. She sees them as opportunities to make friends and learn new things. If people stopped and thought, "What would Dolly do?" I bet so many of the things they think are problems wouldn't be problems anymore.

That's why I think it's super important for kids like us to learn to be more like Dolly. If we grow up putting kindness first, just like her, then maybe when we're grown-ups, the world will be a friendlier place.

Here's a thought, kindness is like a seed. If you plant it, water it, and give it sunshine, it grows into something beautiful. If you're nice to someone, they're more likely to be nice back. And if we all do that, the world will be filled with beautiful kindness flowers.

So let's make a promise to be more like Dolly. Let's be kind, open, and see the good in people. Let's learn to be friends with everyone and never forget how to be kind. If we all act more like Dolly, the world will be a much happier place to live in.

I want to grow up in that world, and I bet you do too!

MY DREAM TO MEET DOLLY

But there's one more thing I want to tell you about, my dreams.

My number one dream, the biggest one of all, is for my dad's kidneys to get better. He's the best dad ever, and he's taught me so much about kindness and love, just like Dolly. I wish every day for his health to improve because he is a great dad and helps others with kidney disease.

My number two dream, right after that, is to one day meet Dolly Parton! Can you imagine how amazing that would be? I hope that maybe, just maybe, Dolly will see this book and reach out to me. I would be the happiest girl in the whole world!

Meeting Dolly would be like meeting a real-life hero. I could thank her for all the beautiful songs, movies, and the joy she's brought into so many lives. I could tell her about how her kindness has inspired me to be a better person. I'd even get to tell her about my dad and how he's just as kind-hearted as she is.

But most of all, I hope that this book will help spread more love and kindness around the world, just like Dolly does. If we can all learn to be more like her, to be open, friendly, and always caring, then the world will be filled with happiness and understanding.

HOW TO BE MORE LIKE DOLLY PARTON

Kindness That Melts Hearts

When we think about Dolly Parton, the first thing that usually comes to mind is her kindness. She has a way of making everyone around her feel special and loved. One real-life example of this is her charity, Dolly Parton's Imagination Library, which gives free books to children. She didn't just donate money, she created a whole program to encourage kids to read and learn.

You can emulate Dolly's kindness in your own life too. For example, do you ever see someone sitting alone at lunch? Why not go over and introduce yourself? You never know, you might make a new friend. Or maybe you could bring an extra pencil or eraser to school to share with someone who needs it. It's the small things that make a big difference.

Understanding is More Than Just Listening

Dolly Parton knows how to relate to people from all walks of life. She listens, understands, and then acts. Being understanding doesn't mean you have to agree with everyone, it just means you're willing to see things from their perspective.

You too can practice understanding in your everyday life. Let's say one of your friends is sad because they didn't do well on a test. Instead of saying, "It's just a test," try to understand their feelings. Maybe that test was really important to them. A simple "I understand why you're upset, how can I help?" can go a long way.

Patience is Golden

In a world that's always in a hurry, patience is a trait that's becoming rare. Dolly Parton didn't become a star overnight, it took years of hard work and patience.

To be more like Dolly, try to build patience in your own life. Remember that good things take time. Whether it's waiting for your turn to speak in a group or being patient with a friend who's going through a tough time, remember that patience is golden.

The Dolly Way of Being Yourself

Dolly Parton has an undeniable feeling of authenticity. She figured out who she wanted to be at a young age and didn't let anyone stop her from becoming that person. Sure, her style and personality may be considered "over the top" by some, but that's who she is. She embraces herself fully, and that has endeared her to people worldwide. Whether it's her vibrant fashion choices or her distinctive southern twang, she is always herself.

You too can learn a lot from Dolly's approach to life. Being authentic means accepting yourself as you are and not changing for anyone else. If you're different, embrace it. If you have unique tastes or interests, celebrate them. Let's say you have a passion for painting but are scared that people might find it "weird." Remember Dolly would tell you to go for it! It might just be this uniqueness that attracts people to you. After all, no one likes a fake person. When you're genuine, people are more likely to respond to you in a positive and authentic manner as well. Being yourself not only makes you happier but also lets you make real connections with others.

Spreading Joy Like Confetti

Dolly Parton has a knack for making people happy wherever she goes. Her songs, her personality, and even her sense of style bring joy to people. One of the ways she does this is by staying positive, even when things are tough.

You can spread joy in the same way! Keep a positive outlook and share it with those around you. Is your friend feeling down about something? Share a funny joke or story to cheer them up. You could also bring a little gift to a friend who needs it or write a positive note to a family member. Remember, joy is contagious. So go ahead, spread it like confetti!

Being more like Dolly Parton is about more than just the clothes and the hair. It's about carrying her spirit of kindness, understanding, patience, and joyfulness with you wherever you go. And you know what? The world could sure use more people like that!

IF YOU SEE SOMEONE WITHOUT A SMILE, GIVE THEM ONE OF YOURS

No matter If you go to school or go to work, If you see someone without a smile, give them one of yours. If you go to school and you see your friend hurt, or just having a bad day, you should talk to them. It doesn't even have to be a friend, if anyone isn't happy, you should help brighten up their day.

School can be a great place to learn and make friends, but sometimes it can also be tough. People might feel left out or sad, or they might even be bullied. I think we can all learn a lot from Dolly Parton about how to make things better.

Be a Good Friend Like Dolly
Dolly Parton always treats people with kindness and

respect. If you see someone at school who looks sad or lonely, try doing what I do on the playground. Walk up to them, introduce yourself, and ask if they want to hang out. Just like Dolly says, "If you see someone without a smile, give them one of yours!"

Stand Up Against Bullying

Bullying is never okay, and Dolly wouldn't stand for it either. If you see someone being bullied, tell a grown-up like a teacher or your parents. If you feel safe, you can also stand up to the bully by telling them to stop. Remember, Dolly believes in love and understanding, so be firm but not mean.

Listen and Be There

Sometimes, all a person needs is someone to listen. If a friend is feeling down, let them know you're there for them. Dolly listens to her fans and cares about them, and we can do the same for our friends. Just being there can make a big difference.

Start a Kindness Club

Why not start a kindness club at school? Get together with friends and come up with ways to spread kindness around your school, like leaving nice notes or helping others. Dolly has her charity that gives away books, so maybe you could organize a book drive or something else that's fun and helpful!

Start a Unique Club

Maybe you want to be more like Dolly and stand out. Why not start a unique club at your school that is fun and different. At my school we have lots of clubs, one is the Lettuce Club. That's right, a club about Lettuce. Who would want to join a Lettuce club? Everyone! The club doesn't sit around and talk about lettuce - they see who can eat a head of lettuce the fastest!

Be Like a Butterfly

Just like Dolly loves butterflies, we can be like butterflies too. A butterfly's gentle touch can make a flower bloom, and your kindness can make someone's day brighter. So be gentle, be kind, and let's make our schools a place where everyone feels welcome.

School should be a place where everyone feels safe and happy. We should always be excited to go to school and see our teachers and friends. By being kind, standing up to bullying, and caring for each other, we can make it just like that. Let's follow Dolly's example and make our schools full of love, kindness, and understanding. Because, in Dolly's words, "The way I see it, if you want the rainbow, you gotta put up with the rain."

THE LITTLE ACTS OF KINDNESS

Have you ever noticed how sometimes the smallest things can have the biggest impact? Just like how a tiny pebble can create big ripples in a pond, our tiny acts of kindness can create huge waves of happiness. Let's look at some simple and awesome ways you can spread kindness everywhere you go.

At Home

1. Wake Up with a Smile
Start the day right. When you wake up, share a cheerful "Good morning!" and a big smile with your family. It sets a positive tone for the day.

2. Be the Family Helper
Notice mom or dad looking tired? Offer to help with chores, like setting the table or tidying up your toys without being asked. They'll really appreciate it!

3. Listen with Your Heart
When someone's sharing a story, put down your toy or game and listen. It shows you care about their feelings and thoughts.

At School

1. Be a Door Hero

If you get to the door first, hold it open. It's a quick and friendly way to say, "I'm here for you!"

2. Show Gratitude

Thank your teachers at the end of a lesson or school day. It's a small thing, but it lets them know they're making a difference.

3. Buddy Bench Pal

Ever see someone sitting alone on the 'Buddy Bench'? Go sit next to them or invite them to play. Everyone needs a buddy now and then.

4. Lend a Hand (or Pencil!)

Always have an extra pencil or eraser? Share with someone who forgot theirs. They'll remember your kindness.

On the Playground

1. Be a Game Changer

Introduce a new game or let someone else pick the game for a change. It's fun to try new things!

2. Always Lend a Helping Hand

If you see someone trip or drop their things, rush over to help them. They'll be grateful, and you might even make a new friend.

3. Swing Shift

When the swings are all taken, and you see someone waiting, offer them a turn. It's a nice way to share the fun!

While Hanging Out with Others

1. Compliment Out Loud

Love those new shoes your friend is wearing? Tell

them! Compliments can light up someone's day.

2. Quick to Apologize

If something goes wrong, even if it was an accident, say "I'm sorry." It shows you're thoughtful and caring.

3. Be a Super Listener

When friends talk about their day, hobbies, or dreams, give them your full attention. Everyone loves feeling heard!

4. Share Your Snacks

Got some extra chips or cookies during lunch? Offer some to those around you. Sharing is a simple way to spread joy.

While these acts might seem small to you, to someone else, they can mean the world. Remember, every act of kindness, no matter how small, can make our world a brighter place. Let's sprinkle kindness everywhere we go!

SHOWING KINDNESS AT SCHOOL

If there's one place we spend a lot of time, it's school. This is where we learn, where we make friends, and where we grow up to be amazing people - like Dolly Parton! She's shown us how important it is to be kind wherever you are. Here's how we can be more like Dolly and keep a sunny outlook at school.

Start the Day with a Smile
Just like Dolly always says, "If you want the rainbow, you gotta put up with the rain." Start each school day with a big smile and a positive thought. Think about something you're looking forward to or a friend you can't wait to see. It'll make the day feel brighter!

Be a Friend to Everyone
Dolly is friends with all kinds of people, and we can be too. Say hi to someone new, sit with someone who's alone at lunch, or give a compliment. Being friendly and kind helps make school a happier place

for everyone, including yourself!

Focus on What You Love

Dolly loves to sing and write songs, and she always gives her best. Find what you love to do at school, whether it's reading, drawing, or playing sports. When you focus on what you love, school becomes more fun.

Ask for Help When You Need It

If something's hard, don't be afraid to ask for help. Dolly never gave up on her dreams, even when things were tough. Talk to your teacher or a friend if you're stuck on something, and you'll feel much better.

Create a Positivity Journal

Why not keep a journal like Dolly might do for her songwriting? Write down good things that happen each day or things you're grateful for. Reading it later will remind you of all the positive things in your life.

Sing a Happy Tune

Dolly loves to sing, and so can you! If you're feeling down, hum or sing your favorite happy song (maybe one of Dolly's!) to lift your spirits.

Remember, You're Special

Dolly always wants us to know that we're unique and special, just the way we are. Believe in yourself, and don't let anyone bring you down. You're amazing, and you can do anything you set your mind to!

Share Your Supplies

We all have those moments when we forget to bring a pencil or when the glue runs out in the middle of an art project. If you have extra supplies, offer them to someone who needs them. It's a small act, but it shows you're thoughtful. This helps create a community feeling in the classroom where everyone helps each other.

Offer to Help Others

Help can come in many shapes and sizes. It could mean helping a classmate understand a math problem or helping the teacher distribute handouts. These acts of service make a big difference and create a positive atmosphere.

Be a Good Listener

Listening is a skill that's often overlooked, but it's one of the best ways to show kindness. If a friend is going through a hard time or if the teacher is giving important instructions, give your full attention. It shows that you respect them and that what they have to say matters to you.

Be Respectful to Teachers

Being respectful to your teachers is a must. Remember, they work hard to help you learn and grow. When you're disrespectful, disruptive, or a distraction, it's not just unkind to the teacher but also to your classmates who are trying to learn. So raise your hand before speaking, listen attentively, and follow the classroom rules. This will make for a more peaceful and productive learning environment for everyone.

Include Everyone
It's super easy to stick with the friends you already have, but think about how you felt when you were the new kid or didn't know anyone. If you see someone sitting alone at lunch or not picked for a team during gym, invite them over. Including others is a simple yet powerful way to spread kindness.

Say Thank You
Gratitude is like magic, it makes everyone feel good. If someone lends you a book, helps you in the classroom, or holds the door for you, a simple "Thank you" goes a long way. It takes just a second to say but can make someone's day.

Be Mindful of Your Words
Ever heard the saying, "If you don't have anything nice to say, don't say anything at all"? It's a good rule to live by. Hurtful words can stick with someone for a long time, so choose what you say carefully.

Give Compliments
Everyone loves to feel recognized and valued. If you notice someone has done well on a test, has a cool new haircut, or just has an amazing smile, tell them! Compliments are a free and easy way to make someone's day.

Celebrate Others' Achievements

If a classmate wins a race, gets a good grade, or achieves something they've been striving for, celebrate with them. It can be as simple as a high-five or a cheerful "Well done!" Being happy for others cultivates a culture of support and mutual respect.

Show Empathy

Sometimes, people around us might be having a tough day. Maybe they missed the bus, forgot their lunch, or just feel down. Offering a listening ear or some comforting words can make a world of difference.

Create a Kindness Jar

Coordinate with your teacher to set up a kindness jar in the classroom. Whenever someone does something kind, they can write it down on a piece of paper and put it in the jar. At the end of each week or month, the teacher can read them aloud. This way, acts of kindness get recognized and celebrated.

Respect School Property

Kindness isn't just about how we treat people, it's also about how we treat our surroundings. By taking good care of the books, desks, and even the walls of the school, you show that you value the space everyone shares.

Help Keep the School Clean

If you see a piece of trash on the ground, pick it up and throw it away. It might not seem like much, but keeping your school clean is a form of respect—to the school and to everyone who studies there.

Write Friendly Notes

A simple note with a positive message can go a long way. Imagine opening your locker and finding a note that says, "You're awesome!" You can make that happen for someone else. Leave a few friendly notes in random places like desks, lockers, or library books.

Support the Underdog

We all know that one person who struggles to keep up in sports, gets nervous while speaking in front of the class, or is shy to the point of invisibility. Lend them your support. A few words of encouragement can boost their confidence immensely.

Offer to Tutor or be Tutored

If you're good at something, offer to help others who are struggling. And if you're the one struggling, don't shy away from asking for help. Learning from each other is one of the best ways to grow, both academically and as people.

Thank Your Bus Driver

Getting to and from school is the first and last part of your school day. A simple "Thank you" to your bus driver shows appreciation for their role in your education.

Be Mindful in the Cafeteria

Lunchtime is a social time, but it's also an

opportunity to show kindness. Invite someone new to sit with you, offer to carry a tray for someone who's struggling, or even just clean up after yourself to make the cafeteria staff's job easier.

JOKES TO HELP MAKE A FRIEND

Making friends can be way easier when you can share a laugh. Jokes are like little gifts of happiness you can give to people. Dolly Parton knows how to use humor to bring joy to people, and so can you! Here's a bunch of kid-friendly jokes that you can use to crack up your friends and make new ones!

Short Jokes:

Why did the scarecrow win an award?
Because he was outstanding in his field!

What do you call fake spaghetti?
An "impasta"!

How do you catch a squirrel?
Climb a tree and act like a nut!

What's orange and sounds like a parrot?
A carrot!

What do you call a bear with no teeth?
A gummy bear!

Why did the bicycle fall over?

Because it was two-tired!

What do you call a cow with no legs?
Ground beef!

What's brown and sticky?
A stick!

Why did the chicken join a band?
Because it had the drumsticks!

How do you make a tissue dance?
You put a little "boogie" in it!

What do you call a pile of cats?
A "meowtain"!

What's a vampire's favorite fruit?
A "necktarine"!

What did one wall say to the other wall?
I'll meet you at the corner!

Why did the math book look sad?
Because it had too many problems!

What kind of tree fits in your hand?
A palm tree!

What has ears but can't hear?
A cornfield!

What's a snowman's favorite snack?
Ice Krispies!

How does a penguin build its house?

Igloos it together!

Why did the tomato turn red?
Because it saw the salad dressing!

What do you call a bear in the rain?
A "drizzly bear"!

What do you call a sleeping bull?
A bulldozer!

What do you call a fish with no eyes?
Fsh!

What's a pirate's favorite letter?
Arrr!

What did the zero say to the eight?
Nice belt!

Knock-Knock Jokes:

Knock, knock.
- Who's there?
- Lettuce.
- Lettuce who?
- Lettuce in, it's cold out here!

Knock, knock.
- Who's there?
- Harry.
- Harry who?
- Harry up and answer the door!

Knock, knock.

- Who's there?
- Cow says.
- Cow says who?
- No silly, cow says "moo"!

Knock, knock.
- Who's there?
- Atch.
- Atch who?
- Bless you!

Knock, knock.
- Who's there?
- Boo.
- Boo who?
- Don't cry, it's just a joke!

Knock, knock.
- Who's there?
- Olive.
- Olive who?
- Olive you and I miss you!

Knock, knock.
- Who's there?
- Tank.
- Tank who?
- You're welcome!

Knock, knock.
- Who's there?
- Orange.
- Orange who?

- Orange you going to let me in?

Knock, knock.
- Who's there?
- Dwayne.
- Dwayne who?
- Dwayne the bathtub, I'm drowning!

Knock, knock.
- Who's there?
- Doris.
- Doris who?
- Doris locked, that's why I'm knocking!

Knock, knock.
- Who's there?
- Radio.
- Radio who?
- Radio not, here I come!

Riddles:

What comes once in a minute, twice in a moment, but never in a thousand years?
- Answer: The letter "M"

What has keys but can't open locks?
- Answer: A piano

What has a neck but no head?
- Answer: A bottle

What comes down but never goes up?
- Answer: Rain

What has one eye but can't see?

- Answer: A needle

What kind of tree can you carry in your hand?

- Answer: A palm

What has a bottom at the top?

- Answer: Your leg

What is so fragile that saying its name breaks it?

- Answer: Silence

What word is spelled incorrectly in every dictionary?

- Answer: Incorrectly

What has an endless supply of letters but starts empty?

- Answer: A mailbox

MAKING FRIENDS

You know, making friends can be like planting a seed and watching it grow into this awesome tree. Except instead of giving you apples or something, it gives you smiles, support, and loads of fun times. I've learned a lot from Dolly Parton about friendships, and trust me, she's the queen of making people feel special. So, grab your notebook, 'cause we're going deep into the world of friendship, Dolly style!

How to Make a Friend

- **Be Yourself**: First off, don't even think about pretending to be someone you're not. Dolly is 100% herself, big hair, sparkly outfits, and all. That's why everyone loves her! If you love comic books, go ahead and geek out. If you love sports, show off that team spirit!
- **Start with Hello**: It sounds basic, I know. But guys, it's like opening the door to a whole new world. One simple 'Hello' led me to meet Savannah and Julia, who are now my go-to people for everything!
- **Show Interest**: This one's important. Ask about their day or what they love to do. Like, if they're really into soccer, ask them about their

favorite team or how they got into the sport. People love to talk about themselves, and it makes them feel special when you listen.

- **Share Something About You**: Don't let it be a one-sided convo. Share something cool or even wacky about you. Friendships are a two-way street!

- **Be Open**: Sometimes we shy away from people who are different, but Dolly says that's not the right thing to do. Being open to making friends with people who are different then you can make your life so colorful!

How to Grow a Friendship

- **Spend Time Together**: Think about it. You won't know if a book is good unless you read it, right? Same with friends. Spend time with them to know them better. Could be watching a movie, having a sleepover, or playing video games.

- **Be Supportive:** If your friend messes up in a game or gets a bad grade, don't join the boo crowd. Be the person who lifts them up.

- **Celebrate the Wins**: Whether it's getting that 'A+' or scoring a goal, be your friend's biggest cheerleader. You could even do a silly victory dance!

- **Be Honest**: If your friend has spinach stuck in their teeth, tell them! Honest friends are for keeps.

- **Have Their Back**: If someone is picking on your

friend, stand up for them. It's what heroes—like Dolly—do!

How to Stay Friends

- **Communication is Key**: If there's drama, don't let it stew. Talk about it. Dolly would probably write a hit song about it, but we can just chat, you know?
- **Be Loyal**: Remember how pirates never leave their treasure? Be like that with your friends. Stick with them through the good and bad, like a true matey!
- **Forgive and Forget**: It's easy to hold a grudge, but hard to carry it. If your friend messes up and says sorry, let it go. Dolly would say, "Holding grudges is like carrying a bunch of heavy rocks."
- **Keep the Fun Alive**: Remember the fun times and try to make more of 'em! Maybe create your own handshake or have a list of must-do adventures.
- **Show Appreciation**: Once in a while, just tell 'em you're glad they're your friend. It could make their whole day, or week, or year!

So there it is, your ultimate guide to making and keeping friends, inspired by the queen of hearts, Dolly Parton! If we all spread a bit of that Dolly kindness, imagine how awesome our world could be. Ready to be a friend superstar?

UNLOCK THE FRIENDSHIP TREASURE CHEST WITH QUESTIONS!

For this chapter we are going to talk about questions. Questions are like the keys to a treasure chest full of friendship gold. Trust me, if you wanna be like Dolly and make tons of friends, you've gotta ask questions. It's how you learn about people and what makes them a good friend for you!

Ice-Breakers (Questions to Start Off)

- **What's Your Favorite Color?** - It's simple, I know, but hey, it's a good opener!
- **Do You Have Any Pets?** - People love talking about their pets. It's like instant friendship juice.
- **What's Your Go-to Snack?** - I mean, who doesn't like talking about food? It's a win-win.
- **What's Your Favorite Subject in School?** - This

can tell you a lot, like if they're a mathlete or a bookworm.

- Do You Play Any Sports? - Great way to find out if you could be teammates or if you'll be cheering them on from the stands.

Going Deeper (More Thoughtful Questions)

- What's Your Dream Vacation? - You might find out you both dream of going to Disneyland or exploring a jungle.
- What's Your Favorite Book? - If it's also your fav, mini high-five! If it's something you haven't read, now you've got a book recommendation.
- Do You Have a Role Model? - Could be their mom, an athlete, or hey, even Dolly!
- What's Your Favorite Way to Relax? - Is it reading? Playing video games? This is the kind of stuff friend dreams are made of.
- What Makes You Laugh the Most? - If it's the same as what makes you laugh, you've struck friendship gold.

Next-Level Friendship (Questions for Close Friends)

- What's Your Biggest Fear? - Big question, I know. But it can bring you guys closer.
- What's the Best Day You've Ever Had? - It's like stepping into a page of their life story.
- How Do You Handle Stress? - This could be a lifesaver during exams or other stressful times.
- What's Your Family Like? - Families are like the backstage crew in the play of our lives, so it's good to know about them.

- What's Important to You in a Friendship? - It's like a friend agreement without all the legal stuff.

There you have it! Questions that can kick off a friendship, make it stronger, or take it to the next level. Remember, Dolly says, "The way I see it, if you want the rainbow, you gotta put up with the rain." So don't be afraid to dive into those questions and dig for that friendship gold.

FUN THINGS TO DO WITH FRIENDS

Friendships are a big deal, and once you've got some cool friends, the next step is having awesome times together. If you're scratching your head thinking of what to do, don't sweat it. I've got a bunch of fun ideas and some tips on how to make sure everyone gets in on the action.

Ideas for Fun Activities

Outdoor Picnic Pick your favorite park and have a picnic. Sandwiches, fruit, and snacks are perfect. Spread out a blanket, and don't forget some music! Eating outside, feeling the breeze—it's an adventure without even traveling!

Movie Marathon Create a cozy spot in the living room, grab snacks, and watch movies all day. Dolly Parton movies, superhero films, or animations—take your pick! Bonus: Try guessing the next scene or dialogue.

Nature Scavenger Hunt Visit your local park and hold a scavenger hunt. Create a list of things to find

—feathers, smooth pebbles, four-leaf clovers. It's an adventure, and the team who finds everything first gets a fun prize!

Craft Day Get your art supplies ready! Spend a day making friendship bracelets, dream catchers, or even simple drawings. Remember the time we all tried to draw our own version of Dolly? Hilarious and so fun!

Bike and Scooter Day Whether you prefer two wheels or a scooter, head out and explore. Design a route around the neighborhood, maybe even have a mini race! Remember safety first: helmets and knee pads.

Cook-Off Challenge Set up your kitchen like a game show. Choose a dish, break into teams, and have a cook-off. Who makes the best spaghetti? Or how about a sandwich-making competition?

Dance and Handshake Day Turn up your favorite songs and dance! You can even create a special handshake. Sage and I created a dance routine that we always giggle about. Memories are made of these moments!

Board Game Bonanza Why play one when you can play three? From strategy games like Risk to simpler ones like Candy Land, let the games begin!

Laser Tag Adventure Whether it's at Zap Zone, Urban Air, or another fun place, laser tag is exciting. Running, hiding, and teaming up—it's like a video game in real life!

Indoor Trampoline Park Visit places like Urban Air and jump away! Whether it's doing flips, bouncing high, or even playing trampoline dodgeball, it's bound to be a lot of fun.

Games That Never Get Old

Charades It's acting without words. Choose a theme —maybe movies or animals—and let the fun begin. The wilder the gestures, the funnier it gets!

Pictionary Drawing without giving verbal clues! Sometimes, the drawings end up being super funny, especially when they look nothing like the word.

Simon Says A game of quick commands. The trick is to only move when "Simon says."

Dodgeball This game is a blast, especially if you're at an indoor trampoline park like Zap Zone. Bouncing and dodging? Double fun!

Hide and Seek Classic game, but ever thought of playing it in the dark using flashlights? It adds a spooky, fun twist!

Card Games Games like Uno, Go Fish, Old Maid, or even making up your own with a simple deck of cards can keep you entertained for hours.

Tag, You're It! A fun, running-around game. Spice it up by creating safe zones where you can't be tagged.

20 Questions Pick an object or a famous person and let others guess by asking only yes-or-no questions. It's a true test of your guessing skills!

Including Shy or Quiet Individuals

Don't forget about the kids who are a bit shy. Sometimes all they need is a friendly invite. Like, "Hey, wanna join us for a game of dodgeball?" You'll be surprised how quickly they come out of their shell.

Remembering Those Often Overlooked

We all know some kids who are always in the background. Maybe they're shy or just like to keep to themselves. But guess what? They want to have fun too! For instance, my cousin Arlynn might be a quiet person, but she's one of the most loving friends you could ever meet.

So that's the rundown. With these activities and games, you're set for some awesome times. The best part is that you're also spreading some of that Dolly kindness by making sure everyone's included. So what are you waiting for? Get out there and have some fun with your friends!

MOVIES AND TV SHOWS TO WATCH WITH FRIENDS

Looking for some epic movies and shows to watch with your buddies? Look no further! I've got a list of 20 awesome picks that are perfect for kids like us, and totally okay for anyone 14 and under.

1. **Wednesday** (on Netflix) Ever heard of the Addams Family? This show's about Wednesday Addams solving a super cool monster mystery at her school. It's mysterious and just plain fun!

2. **Hatchi** Get ready to feel the feels! Hatchi's tale of loyalty and friendship is something special. Don't forget the tissues though! Once when I had something in my eye and needed to cry, my dad played the ending of Hatchi and I was crying instantly. It cleared out what ever was in my eye.

3. **A Dog's Purpose** A movie about a dog's adventures through many lifetimes. It's touching

and makes you think about our pets in a whole new way. This is another one where you need tissues.

4. **Little House on The Prairie** An oldie but a goodie! It's all about life in the old days, with loads of family fun and adventure. For my birthday my dad had the girl who played Nellie Olsen record me a video. I loved it!

5. **Modern Family** This one's just hilarious! A big, wild family and all their super funny stories. Total laugh-out-loud. Lily and Cam are my favorite characters.

6. **The Middle** Life, family, and the funny moments in between. A must-watch if you love a good giggle.

7. **Malcolm in the Middle** Malcolm's family is kinda crazy, but in the best way. Loads of fun and silly moments.

8. **Coco** Amazing music, vibrant colors, and a heartwarming tale about family and dreams.

9. **Toy Story** Toys that come to life? Yes, please! Woody, Buzz, and the gang have some pretty wild adventures.

10. **Mandalorian** (on Disney) For the Star Wars fans! Space, adventure, and a cute little baby Yoda named Grogu.

11. **Trolls** Bright colors, catchy songs, and fun-loving trolls on a mission to save their village. A total jam!

12. **Finding Nemo** A fishy adventure across the ocean. Heartwarming and full of surprises!

13. **The Goldbergs** A family with a dad who yells, a mom who always wants snuggies, and an awesome

grandpa named Pops. Beverly Goldberg likes to sparkle like Dolly and has big hair, but she isn't as friendly as Dolly.

14. **Frozen** Two princess sisters, a snowman, and loads of catchy tunes. You'll be singing along in no time!

15. **The Karate Kid** Learn about determination, hard work, and some cool karate moves. A classic!

16. **Despicable Me** Minions, gadgets, and loads of laughs. Watch as the world's greatest villain turns into the world's greatest dad.

17. **The Incredibles** A superhero family trying to live a normal life? Sounds easy, right? Think again!

18. **Spy Kids** Imagine if your parents were spies and you had to save them. Wild gadgets and loads of action!

19. **Jumanji**: Welcome to the Jungle A video game that comes to life with jungles, animals, and wild challenges. Super fun and exciting!

20. **Harry Potter series** Wizards, magic, and epic battles. Dive into the enchanting world of Hogwarts and see the magic unfold.

So next time you're chilling with friends and wondering what to watch, just pick from this list. Trust me, you won't be bored!

JOINING CLUBS AND TEAMS

When I first heard my mom say, "You and your brother are joining swimming," I was like, "Whaaat?" Swimming wasn't really my thing. I mean, water in my ears, goggles leaving marks on my face, and don't even get me started on the cold water! But here's the cool part: I met some really awesome friends.

Every time we had swimming practice or meets, I'd chat with some kids my age. We'd laugh about the funny faces we make underwater or compete to see who can do the funniest jump into the pool. Slowly, those chat times turned into friendships. We'd hang out after class, have fun pool parties, or even just chat about school and other stuff.

Fast forward to 6th grade. I thought, "Hey, why not try something new?" So, I joined the cross country team. Yep, me, running long distances! It was super tiring at first. My legs would feel like jelly, and I'd be out of breath. But, the more I ran, the more friends I made. We'd cheer for each other, give tips on running, and sometimes even have fun races where we weren't really racing, but just having fun.

Soon, I got to know more about my teammates. Some of them love video games just like me, while others are into books or music. We'd talk about our favorite movies or the coolest songs we've heard lately. It's amazing how running brought us together.

Now, I'm already looking forward to volleyball and track when they start. Not just because of the sports, but because of the friends I'll make. I've realized that joining clubs or teams is like opening a door to a room full of potential friends. And these aren't just any friends, but ones who share the same interests as you.

My advice? If there's a club or team at school or in the community, give it a try! Even if you think it's not your thing, like I thought about swimming, you might end up having a blast. Plus, you'll meet new friends. And guess what? Those friends might introduce you to even more cool stuff and even more awesome people.

DOLLY'S EXPERIENCE WITH BULLYING

Did you know that Dolly Parton had some bad days at school when she was young? She even wrote a song about one time that she was bullied. The song is called "Coat of Many Colors" and it was the first Dolly Parton song my dad taught me.

Dolly Parton's family didn't have much money when she was growing up, but they had lots of love. One day, her mom made her a coat from different pieces of fabric they had gifted to them. It was a beautiful, colorful coat, and Dolly was so proud to wear it. She felt like Joseph from the Bible, who had a coat of many colors too!

But when she wore it to school, some kids laughed at her and made fun of the coat. They didn't see how special it was, they only saw that it was different. Dolly felt hurt and sad, but she remembered her mom's words about how the coat was made with love.

Instead of letting the bullies bring her down, Dolly stood strong and continued to wear her coat with pride. She knew it was special, and she knew she was special too. Later, she wrote a song called "Coat of Many Colors" to tell the story, and it became a big hit!

Dolly Parton didn't let the bullies stop her from being herself. Here's what we can learn from her:

Be Proud of Who You Are
Just like Dolly was proud of her coat, we should be proud of who we are. It's okay to be different!

Stand Up for Yourself
Dolly didn't let the bullies win. If someone is mean to you, tell a teacher or an adult, and remember that you're strong and special.

Remember What's Important
The coat was made with love, and that's what mattered to Dolly. Focus on what's important to you, like family, friends, and being kind.

Learn and Grow
Dolly turned her painful experience into a beautiful song. We can learn from our experiences too and use them to grow stronger and wiser.

Dolly Parton's story of the Coat of Many Colors teaches us to be proud of who we are, even when others don't understand. It's a lesson in love, strength, and the power of believing in ourselves. If we face bullying, we can remember Dolly's wisdom and know that we are special, just the way we are.

HOW TO SPREAD DOLLY KINDNESS

We are all born with kindness in our hearts. Just think about little kids meeting each other for the first time. They don't see differences, they just see a new friend to play with! But as we grow up, sometimes we forget how easy it was to be kind and accepting of others. Life gets more complicated, and we start to see differences instead of similarities. But what if we all stopped and thought, "What would Dolly do?" Dolly Parton always spreads kindness, love, and joy. If we can remember to be more like Dolly, spreading kindness would be just as easy as it was when we were little kids. Here are the 5 things my dad taught me to do to be like Dolly.

1) Use One of Dolly's Encouraging Quotes

Dolly Parton has a way with words that can lift anyone's spirits. One of her quotes that I love is, "If you want the rainbow, you gotta put up with the rain." I like to share her quotes with my friends when they're feeling down. It's a special way to spread Dolly's love and wisdom and remind others that things will get better.

2) Be a Friend to the Lonely

Dolly once saw a girl who was lonely and became her friend. Just like Dolly, I always keep an eye out for kids who look lonely. I'll go over, introduce myself, and invite them to play. You never know how much a new friend can mean to someone. Being a friend is a beautiful way to spread kindness and make the world a brighter place.

3) Even a Little Kindness Can Go a Long Way

Sometimes, something as small as a hug or a smile can make a big difference in someone's day. Dolly teaches us that little acts of kindness add up and can change lives. Whether it's holding the door for someone or saying "thank you," every bit of kindness matters.

4) Be Respectful

Being respectful and polite is another way to show kindness. Dolly always treats others with respect, no matter who they are. A kind word or a simple "please" and "thank you" can change someone's whole day. Let's be like Dolly and show respect to everyone we meet.

5) Accepting People Who Are Different

Dolly teaches us that everyone is special in their own way, and we should accept people for who they are. At my school, I have lots of friends who are different or have disabilities. I know that makes them even more special to have as a friend. My cousin Arlynn has diabetes and Down Syndrome, but she's one of the most loving friends I have. When we visit Cincinnati, I always spend time with Arlynn, and I know she'll always be a great friend.

Spreading Dolly's kindness means being a friend, being respectful, and accepting others, no matter how different they may be. It's about the little things, like using one of Dolly's quotes to encourage someone or giving a hug when it's needed. If we all try to be more like Dolly, we can make the world a better place, one act of kindness at a time.

HOW TO BE ENCOURAGING LIKE DOLLY

These quotes inspire me when I have to do something hard. LIke if I have to do something scary. I'll think about one of her quotes and It will give me the courage to do it. Her quotes inspire others too! Whenever friends and family are sad you can tell them a Dolly quote and 99.9% of the time it will help.

Some of my favorite Dolly quotes

"The way I see it, if you want the rainbow, you gotta put up with the rain."

"If you see someone without a smile give them one of yours"

"You'll never do a whole lot unless you're brave enough to try."

"Find out who you are and do it on purpose."

"Don't get so busy making a living that you forget to

make a life."

"It costs a lot of money to look this cheap!"

"I tried every diet in the book. I tried some that weren't in the book. I tried eating the book. It tasted better than most of the food."

"People always ask me how long it takes to do my hair. I don't know, I'm never there."

"When I'm inspired, I get excited because I can't wait to see what I'll come up with next."

"It's hard to be a diamond in a rhinestone world."

"We cannot direct the wind, but we can adjust the sails."

"I've had to work much harder than a man to get where I am, and that's okay because I know I can outwork them."

"I've always said that I would never do anything to hurt myself, and I won't."

"It's not the load that breaks you down, it's the way you carry it."

"You'll never know how much you have to be thankful for until you've had to fight for it."

HOW DOLLY GOT HER SPARKLING STYLE

Let's talk about how Dolly Parton, who's like the queen of country music, got her epic style. I mean, you just can't imagine Dolly without thinking about those bright, shiny dresses, super high heels, and awesome wigs, right? So, where did it all start? Well, Dolly grew up in a small town in Tennessee. Her family didn't have a lot of money, but they had a lot of love and music.

The Beginning

Dolly's sense of style started when she was just a kid. She was really inspired by a lady in her town who was super confident, even when others judged her. Dolly thought that was really awesome. So, she decided that she was going to be like that too. She didn't let where she came from stop her from being the awesome, shining person she wanted to be.

Be Yourself, Like Dolly

Dolly always says, "Find out who you are, and do it on purpose." That's super smart, and it's helped me, and a ton of other people, be ourselves.

What Do You Like?

If you're trying to figure out what you're all about, think about what you love to do. What's that thing that makes you forget about time? Once you know, make it a big part of your life.

Work for It

Just knowing what you like isn't enough. You've got to work hard to get really good at it. Dolly didn't become a star overnight. She worked super hard for a long time. So, keep at it, and don't give up.

How to Sparkle Like Dolly with Kindness and Confidence

Dolly's not just about looking cool, she's also a super kind and positive person. That's what makes her really sparkle.

Be Kind

Kindness is like a superpower. Just a smile or a nice word can make someone's day a million times better. And kindness is a big deal for Dolly too.

Be Confident

If you walk into a room and you're feeling confident, other people will feel it too. Confidence is kind of like a magnet, it pulls people in.

Stay Positive

In a world where it's easy to be negative, being positive is important. Dolly is always cheerful and hopeful, and that makes her really stand out.

Include Everyone

Last but not least, Dolly is really good at making everyone feel welcome. Like, if you see someone who's all alone, go up to them and say hi. Invite them to join in. You'll be spreading the Dolly sparkle, and maybe even making a new friend.

So, Dolly Parton teaches us that what really makes you shine isn't just what you wear, it's how you act. You don't have to be a famous singer to make a difference. You can sparkle just by being kind, confident, and including everyone. And who knows, maybe you'll inspire someone else to find their sparkle too.

DOLLY'S LOVE FOR READING AND LEARNING

Dolly Parton is known for her incredible talent in singing and acting, but did you know she has a deep love for reading too? When you listen to Dolly's songs, it's like reading a short story because she packs so much feeling and life into her words. That love for language didn't just happen, it's something that she built up by reading and learning all through her life.

Lifelong Learning

Dolly wasn't born with a library full of books. She grew up in a small cabin in the mountains, but she had a vivid imagination. She would read anything she could get her hands on. Dolly's family couldn't afford many books, but they had a Bible, and that was enough to start off her love for reading. In interviews, she often talks about how reading opened up new worlds for her and helped her dream big. Just imagine, a girl from a small town in

Tennessee dreaming to be a star, and look where she is now. She reached for the stars and grabbed them, all while keeping a book in her hand.

Dolly's Imagination Library

Guess what? Dolly loves reading so much that she started her own library called "Dolly Parton's Imagination Library." She didn't just want to enjoy reading by herself, she wanted every kid to get the chance to love books too. Her library program is amazing! It mails free, high-quality books to children from the time they are born until they start school, regardless of their family's income.

My Book in Dolly's Library?

I have this really cool dream: What if this book could be a part of Dolly's library one day? That would be like hitting the jackpot! Just the thought of it fills me with excitement.

Why Dolly's Library is So Important

Reading is more than just looking at words on a page. It helps your brain grow and makes you a more understanding person. There are kids out there who don't have money for the newest books, but Dolly's making sure that's not a roadblock for them. With her Imagination Library, she's helping kids get a strong start on their education and sparking their imaginations.

The Power of A Single Book

One book can change a life. Maybe it's a story about bravery that gives you the courage to face a fear. Or maybe it's a science book that makes you want to become an astronaut. With Dolly's library, kids can have those experiences, just like she did.

Dolly Parton's love for reading and learning is like a blazing fire, warming everyone around her. Through her music and her Imagination Library she spreads the message that reading is magical, that learning is a treasure, and that anyone—from a small-town girl to a world-famous superstar—can achieve great things through the power of books. And hey, you never know, maybe one day the book you're reading right now will end up in Dolly's Imagination Library.

THE IMPORTANCE OF SAYING "I'M SORRY"

Owning up to a mistake and saying "I'm sorry" isn't always a walk in the park. It can be tough. But hey, if Dolly Parton can be as sweet as candy and own up to her mistakes, so can we. Apologizing is important to every true friendship and a sign that you respect the people around you.

The Challenge and Importance of Apologizing

We all know it's not easy to swallow your pride and say "I'm sorry." It can make you feel exposed or maybe even like you're admitting defeat. But let's get something straight: Apologizing actually shows you're strong and thoughtful. It clears the air, heals wounds, and allows both you and your friend to move forward. Remember, no one is perfect, but being able to admit your mistakes is a sign of maturity.

Saying Sorry: The Right Way

If you want to apologize, make sure it's sincere. You might be tempted to quickly mumble "sorry" and hope everyone forgets what happened. But that's not the best way to go. You could write a heartfelt note, apologize in person, or even make a little 'I'm Sorry' card with their favorite colors. Practice what you want to say ahead of time to make sure you express yourself well. The main thing is to make eye contact and speak from the heart. That's the Dolly way!

Beyond Words: Actions Speak Volumes

Sometimes a simple "I'm sorry" doesn't feel like enough. In those cases, you can go the extra mile to show you mean it. How about making your friend's favorite cookies? Or maybe spend some time together doing an activity they love. You can also make a little coupon book of favors you're willing to do for them—anything from helping with homework to setting up their favorite game during recess. Small actions like these can add a lot of weight to your apology.

Saying Sorry to Parents: A Special Case

Let's not forget, parents appreciate apologies too! When you mess up at home, a heartfelt apology can make a big difference. To really show your parents you're sorry, consider doing a chore that you know they'd appreciate without them even asking. Could be as simple as washing the dishes, sweeping the porch, or even tidying up the living room. This shows you're thinking about how your actions affect them, which is a super grown-up thing to do.

When you make a mistake, it's like accidentally tripping and causing a vase to fall. Saying "I'm sorry" is the first step, then picking up the pieces. It shows that you recognize your actions have consequences and you want to make things better. So, the next time you're in a tricky spot, ask yourself: What would Dolly do? I bet she'd give a heartfelt apology and try to make things right, proving once again why she's such an amazing role model for all of us.

THE POWER OF FORGIVENESS

Forgiveness is like a superpower. It's a tough thing to do, but it's so important for our happiness and peace of mind. Holding onto anger and grudges can make us feel heavy, like we're carrying around a big, ugly backpack full of rocks. But when we forgive, it's like setting that heavy backpack down. Ahh, feel the relief?

You see, nobody's perfect. We all make mistakes, and guess what? We'll keep making them. That's just part of being human. Holding a grudge is like trapping ourselves in a never-ending cycle of bad feelings. It doesn't just hurt the person who did something wrong, it hurts us, too. And hey, if we expect others to forgive us for our slip-ups, shouldn't we do the same for them?

The Grown-Up Choice: Being Mature About Mistakes

When someone messes up, it's easy to get upset. But showing that you're mature means understanding that mistakes happen. Sometimes we say stuff we don't mean, or do things without thinking. But that's not the whole story of who we are. The mature thing to do is to talk about it, say sorry if we're the ones who goofed up, and move on. You'll feel like a weight has been lifted off your shoulders. Plus, people will respect you for being mature and forgiving.

Ways to Show You've Forgiven Someone
So, how can you show that you've forgiven someone? Well, words are a good start. Simply saying "I forgive you" is super powerful. But actions speak louder than words, so here are some ways to really show you've moved on:

1. Be Kind: Yep, kindness again. It always wins. Show them through your actions that you've moved past the issue.
2. Hang Out: If it's a friend who messed up, invite them to do something fun. It'll show them you're not holding onto bad feelings.
3. Help Them Out: If they're going through a tough time, be there for them. It'll show you've really let go of the past.
4. Be Yourself: Sometimes the best way to show you've forgiven someone is to act like you always have. Keep being the awesome you.

What About Big Mistakes?
Alright, so what if the thing they did is really, really bad? That's a tough one. Sometimes things happen

that make us so mad or hurt that it feels impossible to forgive. In these times, it might take a while. And that's okay. Forgiveness doesn't mean you have to forget what happened or act like it was no big deal. It just means you're choosing to move on for your own peace and happiness.

Your Task: Practice Forgiveness
Here's your challenge: The next time someone hurts your feelings or messes up, take a deep breath. Before reacting, ask yourself: Is holding a grudge going to make this situation better? Most times, you'll find that forgiveness is the best path forward. So, take off that heavy backpack and feel the freedom of forgiveness!

HOW I MET SOME OF MY FRIENDS

Making friends might seem like a tricky puzzle sometimes. But using the tips I recommend in this book can help unlock the secrets to creating lasting friendships. Here are some stories about how I met some of my closest pals!

Savannah

Moving can be scary. New house, new school, and the idea of making new friends can seem scary. But as we were moving into our new home, I saw a chance to make a friend. Savannah was outside, probably curious about her new neighbors. I worked up the courage, walked up to her, and introduced myself. Like a scene out of a movie, we clicked instantly! We shared stories, laughs, and dreams. Fast forward to today, we're still inseparable even 275 miles apart, and it's been nearly seven years! The bonus? Savannah introduced me to **Julia** and **Samantha,** expanding our circle of friendship.

Sage

One day, as the sun was shinning brightly, I was

walking my dog Amsterdam with my mom when a colorful snow cone stand caught my eye. Behind the stand was a girl with a bright smile, selling snow cones. How could I resist? As I approached, I introduced myself and, of course, got myself a refreshing snow cone. Turns out, Sage and I had so much in common! We went to the same school, both were swimmers, and our birthdays were super close. Destiny? I think yes!

Lydia

Starting at a new school can be nerve-wracking. All those unfamiliar faces and figuring out where you fit in. But on the very first day, as I walked into my classroom, I was greeted with a friendly face. Lydia was seated right next to me, and by the time lunch rolled around, we had shared stories, snacks, and even some inside jokes. But Lydia didn't stop at just being my friend, she became the link to meeting many others. Through her, I met **Emma**, **Layla**, **Leah**, and **Juliet.** Each of them unique, each of them special.

Josie

Playing outside always brings back the best memories. Fresh air, fun games, and sometimes, a new friend. One day, as I was playing by our stream, I spotted another girl about my age. It was Josie. We started talking about everything under the sun. We laughed at the silliest things and connected over shared interests. The best part? Josie lives just three doors down from me. The benefit of having a friend so close is great!

These stories aren't just about how I met my friends, but about taking the chance and reaching out. The world is full of possible friends, all it takes is a simple "hello." So, next time you find yourself in a new place or situation, remember my stories and take that leap. It might just lead to a lifelong friend!

KINDNESS TO ANIMALS: WHY EVERY CREATURE MATTERS

Do you know what's just as important as being kind to people? Being kind to animals! Every animal, from the biggest elephant to the tiniest ant, deserves kindness and love.

Growing up, my house was always filled with the happy sounds of animals. My parents have such big hearts and always tried to help animals in need. Can you believe we fostered dogs until they found a family to love them forever? My mom even babysat pets for people while they were at work or away on a trip. We've always had at least two dogs of our own in our home. Having furry friends around is like having extra family members who are always there to play and cuddle.

Playing with animals is one of my favorite things to do. I mean, who doesn't love holding a soft bunny or playing fetch with a playful dog? But, it's super important to remember that animals have feelings too. Even when they do something naughty, like when our new dog Gracie chewed up a fidget toy, it's important to be patient and kind. They're still learning, just like us!

One of the most exciting trips I take every year is to Berlin, Ohio. It's an Amish area, and guess what? It's like an animal paradise! Each visit is an adventure. I get to help with feeding and caring for so many animals. There's always something new to learn and some new friends to meet. And the best part? We have annual passes to one of the most massive petting zoos there! It's our daily ritual to visit it twice a day, almost every single day we're there.

One of my favorite memories is holding baby animals. I once held a baby pig, a baby goat, and even one-day-old ducks! Can you imagine how soft and cute they were? I felt so lucky to be trusted with such tiny, precious creatures.

That's not all. Another farm offers a super cool wagon ride. Imagine being on a wagon and getting to pet and feed Zebras, Water Buffalos, Deer, Giraffes, Pigs, Buffalo, and more! It feels like a real-life safari adventure. We have been there twice in 2023, and I can't wait for our next trip.

Thinking about my future, I've wondered if I should be a vet or maybe train police dogs in the Air Force. It's a big dream, but with my love for animals, I think

I could do it.

Now, did you know that Dolly Parton also loves animals? That's right! Just like how she sings and brings joy to people, she also believes in spreading kindness to animals. She understands that every creature has a heart and feelings.

If you're looking to be kind to animals, here are some ways:

- Always give them fresh water and good food.
- Make sure they have a cozy place to sleep.
- Spend time with them, playing or just sitting together.
- If an animal is scared or hurt, approach gently with an adult's permission and speak in a soft voice.

Remember, animals can't tell us in words if they're sad or in pain. So, we have to watch for signs and be their voice. Every time we show love to an animal, we make the world a better place.

It's not just about pets, though. Even wild animals deserve respect. If you see a squirrel or a bird while you're out and about, give them space and enjoy watching them from a distance.

But guess who else is a massive fan of animals? Dolly Parton! Just like she fills the world with her songs and stories, she believes in showering love on animals. She knows that every creature, big or small, has feelings, and they deserve all our kindness.

Being kind to animals is not just about feeding them or petting them. It's about understanding their feelings, giving them space when they need it, and always being gentle. Whether it's a pet, a farm animal, or even a wild animal we spot during our outdoor adventures, every animal has its own story. And by showing them kindness, we become a part of that story.

So, the next time you meet an animal, remember to be gentle, be kind, and be loving. After all, in a world where we can be anything, let's choose to be kind. And as Dolly would say, if we want the rainbow, we have to deal with a little rain. Let's promise to be rainbows in the lives of these animals, showering them with colors of love and joy.

MAKING POTATO CANDY

Guess what? Potato candy is one of the coolest things ever! My Grandma Fabin makes it and it's the best. It might sound weird at first because it's candy made from potatoes, but trust me, it's super tasty. Every time Grandma Fabin makes it, I can't wait to eat some and share with my friends. They always look at me funny when I first tell them what it is, but then they try it and totally get why I love it so much.

And here's something even more awesome: Dolly Parton, the famous singer, used to eat potato candy when she was a kid too! They even have it at Dollywood, her theme park. How cool is that? A candy that's both in my kitchen and a famous place!

Okay, now I'm going to tell you how to make this candy. Get ready to make something really yummy!

Ingredients:
- 1 small potato (about the size of an egg)
- 4 to 5 cups of powdered sugar (you might need more or less, so have extra on hand)
- 2 teaspoons vanilla extract
- 1/4 teaspoon salt
- 1/4 cup peanut butter (smooth or crunchy, based on your preference)

Instructions:

1. Prepare the Potato: Peel the potato and cut it into chunks. Place the chunks in a saucepan with enough water to cover them. Bring to a boil and cook until the potato is tender.
2. Mash the Potato: Once cooked, drain the water and mash the potato in a large bowl until smooth. Let it cool a little so it's just

warm to the touch.

3. Add Powdered Sugar: Begin by adding about two cups of powdered sugar to the mashed potato, along with the vanilla extract and salt. Mix it all together. The mixture will become liquidy at first, but that's okay!

4. Continue to Add Powdered Sugar: Keep adding more powdered sugar, half a cup at a time, and mix it in. You'll want to achieve a doughy consistency, similar to cookie dough. Depending on the size of the potato, you might need more or less powdered sugar.

5. Rolling Out the Dough: Dust a clean surface with powdered sugar. Turn out the dough onto this surface and roll it out into a rectangle that's about 1/4 inch thick.

6. Spread Peanut Butter: Evenly spread the peanut butter over the surface of the rolled-out dough.

7. Roll It Up: Starting from one end, gently roll the dough into a log, like you would with cinnamon rolls.

8. Chill: Place the log in the refrigerator for at least 2 hours, or until it's firm.

9. Slice and Serve: Once chilled, have your parents use a sharp knife to slice the log into 1/2-inch pieces.

And there you have it! Delicious and unique potato candy. Remember, it's really sweet, so a little goes a long way. Enjoy sharing it with friends and family!

THINKING
LIKE DOLLY

Kind people always think about how what they say and do affects other people. Here's how I imagine Dolly thinks before she says or does something:

1. Is it Kind? Before doing anything, Dolly probably asks herself, "Is this a kind thing to do?" She knows that kindness is like a superpower, and she always wants to use it.

2. Will it Help Someone? Dolly loves to help people. Just think about her book program that gives free books to kids! She always thinks about how she can make someone's day better.

3. Listen First, Speak Later. Dolly knows that to really understand someone, you need to listen to them. By listening, you learn so much about what someone's going through.

4. Stay True to Yourself. Even though Dolly is a big star, she never forgot where she came from. She stays true to who she is and always remembers her roots. That's

important because being genuine is a big part of kindness.

5. Share the Joy. Whether it's her music, her stories, or just a smile, Dolly loves to share happiness. When you share joy, it's like spreading sunshine on a cloudy day.

If someone's not being nice, remember one of Dolly's quotes, like,"We can't direct the wind, but we can adjust the sails." Don't let them bring you down from your Dolly spirit. I hope you can help spread kindness. Spreading kindness is not only kind, but it also feels good when you can say that you did something kind today.

Just remember, what would the best singer in the world do?

A BIG THANK YOU!

You did it! You read through the whole book. That's pretty awesome! First off, I want to say a big **THANK YOU** for spending time with my words and ideas. It means so much to me!

You know, when I started writing this book, I had one big wish. I hoped that anyone who read it would learn how to be kinder, make some amazing friends, and be an all-around great person. And guess what? If you've read this far, I bet you're on your way to doing just that.

Dolly Parton is such an inspiration for me. She's kind, she's funny, and she always tries to make the world a better place. I hope that by reading my book, you feel inspired to be a little more like Dolly in your own life.

Remember, it's the small things that count. A smile, a hello, or just being there for someone can make a big difference. So, keep spreading kindness, making friends, and just being the awesome person you are.

Thanks again for reading, and I hope you have a super amazing day!

Your friend,
Kennadee

Made in the USA
Columbia, SC
18 December 2023

28897750R00065